L 5.1
P 05

Festivals of the *World*

ITALY

Gareth Stevens Publishing
MILWAUKEE

5000447 Italy

Written by
ELIZABETH BERG

Designed by
HASNAH MOHD ESA

Picture research by
SUSAN JANE MANUEL

First published in North America in 1997 by
Gareth Stevens Publishing
1555 North RiverCenter Drive, Suite 201
Milwaukee, Wisconsin 53212 USA

For a free color catalog describing Gareth
Stevens' list of high-quality books and multimedia
programs, call
1-800-542-2595 (USA)
or 1-800-461-9120 (Canada).
Gareth Stevens Publishing's Fax: (414) 225-0377.
See our catalog, too, on the World Wide Web:
http://gsinc.com

© **TIMES EDITIONS PTE LTD 1997**
Originated and designed by
Times Books International
an imprint of Times Editions Pte Ltd
Times Centre, 1 New Industrial Road
Singapore 536196
Printed in Singapore

Library of Congress Cataloging-in-Publication Data:
Berg, Elizabeth.
Italy / by Elizabeth Berg.
p. cm. — (Festivals of the world)
Includes bibliographical references and index.
Summary: Describes how the culture of Italy is
reflected in its many festivals, including Carnival,
various Saints' days, and the Venice Regatta.
ISBN 0-8368-1934-9 (lib. bdg.)
1. Festivals—Italy—Juvenile literature. 2 Italy—
Social life and customs—Juvenile literature.
[1. Festivals—Italy. 2. Italy—Social life and
customs.] I. Title. II. Series.
GT4852.A2B47 1997
394.26945—dc21   97-9842

1 2 3 4 5 6 7 8 9 01 00 99 98 97

CONTENTS

It's Festival Time . . .

The Italians call it a *festa*, but whatever you call it, get ready for a good time. We'll take in a horse race, then put on masks and go to a masked ball. And when we get hungry, we'll stop for pizza. Want to see some knights in shining armor? How about going to a ball game? Come on, join the fun. It's festa time in Italy . . .

WHERE'S ITALY?

I taly is a small country. It occupies a **peninsula** shaped like a boot that juts out from the southern coast of Europe into the Mediterranean Sea. Most of the country is covered with hills or mountains, including the Alps in the north, which are the highest mountains in Europe. It also includes the two large islands of Sicily and Sardinia.

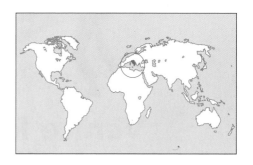

Who are the Italians?

Through its long history, Italy has had a big influence on the rest of the world. The Romans spread their language and culture all over Europe. During the **Renaissance**, painters like Michelangelo and Leonardo da Vinci created works of art that are still admired everywhere. But Italy has only been a country for a little over 100 years. Before that, it was divided into many small states that fought with each other. Even today, Italians are often most loyal to their city—or sometimes their neighborhood! Almost all Italians are Catholics.

An Italian boy. The Italians come from a mixture of many different people.

Map labels

SWITZERLAND
AUSTRIA
SLOVENIA
FRANCE
Ivrea
Venice
CROATIA
BOSNIA HERZEGOVINA
Genoa
ALPS
MONACO
Viareggio
Florence
ADRIATIC SEA
LIGURIAN SEA
Siena
Corsica
ROME
TYRRHENIAN SEA
Naples
SARDINIA
Cagliari
IONIAN SEA
MEDITERRANEAN SEA
Palermo
Trapani
SICILY
ALGERIA
TUNISIA
ITALY
N

A **gondola** passes under the Rialto Bridge in Venice. Venice is built around a network of canals.

WHEN'S THE FESTA?

SPRING

- ✪ **CARNIVAL**
- ✪ **ST. JOSEPH'S DAY**—There are religious plays and parades in honor of the patron saint of Palermo in Sicily.
- ✪ **LIBERATION DAY**—Celebrates the liberation of Italy at the end of World War II.
- ✪ **ST. MARK'S DAY**
- ✪ **HOLY WEEK**
- ✪ **EASTER**—In Florence during Easter mass, a mechanical dove is sent down from the High Altar to a cart filled with fireworks. It sets off the fireworks.

I'm all ready for the Joust of the Saracen. But how will I be able to see where I'm going?

SUMMER

- ✪ **ST. EFISIO'S DAY**
- ✪ **ST. ANTHONY'S DAY**
- ✪ **FEAST OF ST. JOHN THE BAPTIST**
- ✪ **FEAST OF THE REDEEMER**—A bridge of boats and picnics on the water celebrate the end of a **plague**. In the evening, there are fireworks over St. Mark's Church.
- ✪ **PALIO**
- ✪ **ASSUMPTION OF THE VIRGIN**—People buy crickets in cages in the marketplace and set them free as night falls.

I'm La Befana. You'd better hope I don't bring you coal on Epiphany!

AUTUMN

⭐ **JOUST OF THE SARACEN**—Horsemen try to ride past and hit a target.

⭐ **FESTIVAL OF THE LANTERNS**—Children run through the streets with lanterns to celebrate the birth of the Virgin.

⭐ **ST. GENNARO'S DAY**—Every year in Naples, St. Gennaro's blood is brought out of the church, and everyone watches as it miraculously liquefies.

⭐ **MAROSTICA CHESS GAME**—People dress up in costumes from the Middle Ages and play a living chess game.

⭐ **THRUSH FESTIVAL**—Grilled thrush is served on the piazza to celebrate this little bird.

⭐ **ALL SAINTS' DAY**—The dead leave their tombs and raid the pastry shops to bring treats to the children.

WINTER

⭐ **ST. LUCY'S DAY**

⭐ **CHRISTMAS**—Many people create big nativity scenes. This was started by St. Francis, who asked an artist to create a manger scene.

⭐ **EPIPHANY**—Naughty children dread Epiphany, when La Befana brings coal (it's really candies that look like coal) to naughty children and presents to good children. La Befana was a woman who said she was too busy to come with the Wise Men when they went searching for the Christ Child. She has regretted it ever since and so brings gifts to children every year.

PALIO IN SIENA

Seventeen silk flags hang from the arched windows of the town hall. It is an afternoon in August in the main square of Siena. The six mace bearers of the city slowly march past the town hall. Next come the standard bearers for the neighborhoods of the city, musicians, more flag bearers, and guards and pages. Then come the participants, dressed in costumes from the Middle Ages. Each wears the color of his or her neighborhood group, called a *contrada* [cone-TRAH-dah]. At the end of each contrada comes the jockey, and finally the all-important horse. All hopes rest on this horse, which in the following days will prove either the glory or the shame of the contrada. This is Palio, to you perhaps just a horse race, but to the citizens of Siena the most important day of the year.

Flag bearers do many tricks with the flags. As they pass the archbishop, the flag bearers throw up their flags and catch them in a stunning display.

What contrada do you belong to?

As the procession moves along, the air is filled with confetti.

To the Sienese, it is very important to be a good member of a contrada. You are part of the contrada where you were born, and you always return to the contrada to celebrate the important events in your life. Each contrada has its own symbol, its own church, its own patron saint, its own motto, and its own flag. It is like a big family. And every year, you go out and cheer for your contrada during Palio, because to win the Palio is what every contrada hopes for.

Here's a knight in shining armor walking in the Palio procession. This is how real knights looked in Italy centuries ago.

Getting ready to win

Preparations for the race begin weeks ahead of time. While adults try to strike a bargain that will help their horse win, young contrada members spend the evenings walking the streets singing songs of praise to their horse and shouting contrada fight songs. The day before the race, the horse is taken to the neighborhood church to be blessed by the priest. If he relieves himself in the church, people consider it very lucky. (The horse is more important than the jockey, since once in awhile a horse without a rider wins the race.) The night before the race, all 400 or 500 members of the contrada have a big feast on the neighborhood *piazza* [pee-AT-za], where they eat and drink and sing the night away.

During the Palio horse race, the jockeys ride bareback.

Think about this
Palio takes place twice a year. The larger one is on the day after the Assumption of the Sacred Virgin, who is the patron saint of Siena. In Italy, religious holidays can sometimes be pretty wild and crazy. But then, Halloween is a religious holiday, too, and that's not very serious.

Young contrada members wearing their contrada colors and ready for the race.

The victory party goes on all night long—and for days, even months, afterward.

Palio

Finally, after weeks of anticipation, it's time for the race. The procession finishes its slow progress; all the contradas finish filing past. Drums roll and trumpets blast to announce the race. Young members of the contradas try to out-sing each other in support of their horse. In two minutes, the horses run three times around the Campo, the main square in Siena. Many horses fall down as they go around the sharp curves. Once the race is over, the winners keep the victory banner. *Palio* means "banner." The winning contrada's flag hangs alone from the window of the town hall, and an all-night party begins in the winners' neighborhood. The others must wait until next year for their chance at glory.

11

CARNIVAL

Imagine walking along a canal on a cold February morning in Venice. As you walk, you meet a group of clowns all dressed alike. Then a sun walks by, dressed in all the colors of the rainbow. A princess hurries across the bridge, leading someone in a bear costume. Everyone you pass seems to be wearing a mask. There are so many costumes, and they are all so colorful. It's Carnival time.

The last party

Carnival is an old Catholic festival. It celebrates the last day before the 40-day fast of Lent, when Catholics traditionally gave up eating during the daylight hours. Carnival comes from the Latin words *carne levarem*, which means "farewell to the flesh." In the old days, it was a time to have one last party before Lent. But Venetians liked to party in those days, and their Carnival celebrations went on for months, starting from before Christmas.

Left: People spend weeks making their costumes for Carnival. Each one is a work of art.

Above: A painted face for Carnival.

Opposite: A couple stands on one of the many bridges of Venice. The man wears the **maschera nobile** [mas-KA-rah NO-bee-lay], or noblemen's mask. That's the traditional costume for Carnival.

Sir Mask

The biggest part of Carnival in Venice is the costumes. For a day, Venice is changed into a dream world. In the old days, Carnival was an even bigger celebration. Everyone had to wear a mask. And everyone called each other **Sior Maschera** [see-OR mas-KA-rah], or Sir Mask, whether they were a man or a woman or a prince or a servant. Everyone was equal during Carnival.

Have you seen this Pierrot costume before? This is a character that was invented in Italy long ago.

A battle of oranges

In the small mountain town of Ivrea, people board up their windows when Carnival time comes around. Why? Well, you don't want your living room to be covered with squashed oranges, do you? On Sunday, Monday, and Tuesday afternoons of Carnival week, the piazzas in the old section of town turn into a battlefield. Hundreds of foot soldiers defend themselves from cartloads of warriors armed with oranges. The fighting is fierce. The town and all the participants end up covered with orange juice, pulp, and peels.

Think about this
Do you know of any other Carnival celebrations? Are they similar to Carnival in Venice? How are they different?

Two people dressed as Death bother a poor victim.

Opposite: In Viareggio, there are big parades with huge floats. The floats often make fun of well-known people, showing them as devils.

HOLY WEEK IN SICILY

Christmas is a big holiday in Sicily, but bigger still is Holy Week. In some towns, there is a procession on Easter Sunday to celebrate Christ's **resurrection**. In other towns, Good Friday is the most important day. These towns celebrate by putting on a drama of the **crucifixion**. The little town of Trapani is famous for its Good Friday procession. For 400 years, the procession of the "Mysteries" has taken place every year on Good Friday.

The Trapani Mysteries

At two o'clock on Friday afternoon, trumpets and drums announce the procession. First comes the **confraternity** of San Michele, dressed in red tunics with white hoods. Behind them come the Mysteries, 20 groups of life-sized statues showing scenes from the death of Christ. Each is carried on a platform by as many as 24 men from one of the **trade guilds**—the fishermen carry the scene of the washing of the disciples' feet, while the carpenters carry the crucifixion. At the end comes the Virgin Mary, behind dozens of mourning women dressed all in black.

One of the Trapani Mysteries. A band playing sad music walks along with each scene.

A long night

All night long the procession slowly winds through the streets of Trapani. In the early hours of the morning, weary from the long night's march, they approach the Church of the Purgatorio. But as they come up to the door, they hesitate. Back and forth they go, hesitating to enter the church. The excitement builds. Finally, they decide to enter. Last to go in is the Virgin Mary. As she approaches the church, red and white flower petals shower down on her. After much hesitation, she too finally enters the church, and the door closes behind her.

The procession starts from the church.

Sicilians are deeply religious. For many people, the Good Friday procession is a very emotional experience.

17

Chocolate eggs

A long time ago, people used to break their fast for Lent by eating hard-boiled eggs. Later, Italians started dying the eggs by wrapping them in herbs or flowers. Onion skins turn the egg golden, while violets turn it lavender. Then they got the idea of making chocolate eggs, wrapping them up in brightly colored foil, and decorating them with bows and ribbons. Some are very tiny, others huge. All of them are hollow, and all of them have some little present or surprise inside. Sometimes people put very special surprises inside, like diamond rings or airplane tickets. One year, 10 million pounds of chocolate were used to make Easter eggs!

These women are getting ready for the Easter parade in Piana degli Albanesi. The women wear sparkling green and red costumes and headdresses covered with jewels. After the parade, red-dyed eggs are given out to everyone.

Celebrating life

In San Fratello, the Easter celebration is more like a Carnival. People dress as red devils with black leather tongues, horse tails, and trumpets. They are supposed to represent Christ's murderers, and in the past, they would beat themselves with whips to show their sorrow. Today, they walk the streets, singing loudly and acting crazy. Before Christianity came to Italy, springtime was a time for wild parties celebrating the renewal of life after the end of winter. Italian celebrations of Holy Week often continue many of the same traditions. In Christ's death and resurrection, Italians once again celebrate the coming to life of the earth after its winter death.

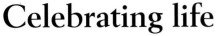

Think about this
Holy Week celebrations continue many traditions that celebrate the coming of life in spring. In Trapani, sprouted seeds are put on display in the church on Thursday of Holy Week.

San Fratello's red devils add some fun to the Easter festivities.

SAINTS' DAYS

Every day is a saint's day in Italy. The Catholic Church has a saint for every day of the year. And for every saint, there is sure to be a town in Italy that claims him or her as its patron saint. But you never know how the townspeople are going to celebrate their patron saint's day. It could be a solemn day of religious processions, or it could be a football game.

A statue of St. Anthony of Padua is carried in a procession on his feast day. In Rome, people bring their horses and mules to the church to be blessed.

Pick a saint

Who's your favorite saint? Is it St. Anthony, the patron saint of careless people? If you've lost something important, you might celebrate St. Anthony's Day on June 13th. Or maybe you prefer St. Mark. On April 25th, St. Mark's Eve, women and girls get a rosebud from their admirers. You'd probably like St. Lucy's Day, when everyone eats a special candy. Legend says that St. Lucy's donkey likes these so much that he stops and leaves presents for the children at every house where candies are left outside.

Come to Sardinia

On the island of Sardinia, the big celebration is for St. Efisio's Day. St. Efisio is the patron saint of Cagliari, the capital city. On May 1st, the anniversary of the day he was **martyred**, there is a big procession. The mayor of Cagliari leads the way on a white horse. Musicians follow, playing Sardinian flutes. Next comes the statue of St. Efisio, glittering in its rich robes and jewels, on a beautiful cart. The priests follow, and behind them are thousands of people in the costumes of their villages.

On St. Efisio's Day, oxcarts decorated with garlands of flowers start out from Cagliari and slowly travel along the bay until they reach the beach where the saint was killed.

People of Sardinia in traditional dress for St. Efisio's Day.

The Feast of St. John

The patron saint of Florence is St. John the Baptist. For his day, Florentines have a big procession of drummers, flag bearers, soldiers, and nobles on horseback, all dressed in costumes from the **Middle Ages**. After the procession, teams from the different areas of the city play a kind of football game—a very rough one. Each team has its own traditional medieval costume, either white, blue, red, or green. You can hit or bite the other players, and players sometimes get badly injured. The games go on for three days. Then it all finishes with a big fireworks display and an all-night party in the winners' neighborhood.

Left: A flag bearer wears a costume from the Renaissance.

Above: The winner's prize, a beautiful white cow, is led in the procession.

But that's not all

That's the way Florentines celebrate St. John's Day. In Genoa, 50 confraternities take their boats out to sea for a beautiful parade on the water. In other towns, there are other water celebrations for St. John's Day, like diving into the sea three times in memory of St. John's baptism of Christ. The Feast of St. John also happens to fall very close to Midsummer's Day, when the days start to grow shorter. Before Christianity came to Italy, Midsummer was celebrated with bonfires. On St. John's Eve, the little village of Grello brings back these ancient fire customs. Teams of teenagers race through the fields with blazing straw brooms. At the end, the winners have the honor of lighting the bonfire. Then special foods are grilled on the piazza, and everyone has a big feast.

Think about this

Do you celebrate any saints' days? Do you give valentines for Valentine's Day? St. Valentine was a Roman priest who was killed because of his beliefs. The reason you celebrate his day with valentines is because in ancient Rome February 14th was known as Lupercalia, a festival in honor of young lovers.

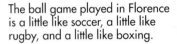

The ball game played in Florence is a little like soccer, a little like rugby, and a little like boxing.

VENICE REGATTA

Venice is a city of canals. Instead of streets, there are canals. If you lived in Venice, you would probably take a boat to school, and your mom would take a boat to go shopping. Venetians use a special type of boat, called a gondola. The person who rows the boat is called the gondolier. Canals are so important to Venice that there are several festivals on the water. Would you like to come to a boat race? Join us for the Venice Regatta.

A band in costume plays on one of the boats.

Let's go sailing

The regatta begins with a historical procession of boats and barges. All the crew members wear costumes from long ago. Afterward, there is a series of rowing races up the Grand Canal. The Grand Canal is the big canal that runs through the center of Venice. Boats are part of many Venetian festivals. During the Feast of the Redeemer, boats line up across a canal to let people walk across to the Church of the Redeemer. This festival celebrates the end of a terrible plague.

Opposite: The procession of old boats sails up the Grand Canal. The striped poles you see are for people who live along the canal to tie up their boats. Would you like to live in one of these houses?

THINGS FOR YOU TO DO

On the third Sunday in June, the little town of Spello celebrates Corpus Christi by making pictures out of flowers. But these are no ordinary pictures—they take up the entire street leading up to the cathedral. The preparations start a year in advance. Teams get together to draw plans of the picture they will make. Then, two weeks before the big day, they pick the flowers they will need.

Making the pictures

Around three o'clock on Saturday afternoon, the street is closed to traffic. Groups of teenagers carefully start to lay out the flower petals. Slowly, a madonna and child take shape on one section of the road, while on another, God leans down from a cloud. The artists work all night long. By nine o'clock in the morning, all the pictures are finished, and all the people of the town turn out to look at the works of art. Then the procession begins. The bishop steps out of the cathedral onto the carpet of flowers. He walks the length of the street, scattering the flowers. He is followed by priests, a marching band, and a crowd of others. Soon there are flower petals blowing all over the town.

Try it yourself

Try making your own flower picture. You could, of course, do it on the walkway in front of your house and let the flowers blow away. Or you could make something more permanent, but a little less authentic. Cut out some petals from sheets of colored paper. Cut them in different shapes, just like real flowers. Then draw a picture onto a piece of cardboard. Glue the "petals" to the cardboard to make your picture.

Things to look for in your library

A Taste of Italy. Jenny Ridgwell (Thomson Learning, 1993).

The Canary Prince. Eric Jon Nones (Farrar Straus & Giroux, 1991).

Caterina, the Clever Farm Girl: A Tuscan Tale. Enzo Giannini, Julienne Paterson (Dial Books for Young Readers, 1996).

The Christmas Witch. Joanne Oppenheim (Gareth Stevens, 1997).

Italy. (Barr Films).

Italy. (Journal Films and Video).

Italy: Country Topics for Craft Projects. Rachel Wright, Teri Gower, Patricia Borlenghi (Franklin Watts, 1995).

Italy: Games People Play. Miles Harvey (Children's Press, 1996).

MAKE A CARNIVAL MASK

Venetians put a lot of work into their masks for Carnival. Every one is different. Here's an idea for a mask to make for your own Carnival celebration. If you want, you can add your own touches to make it unique!

1

2

4

3

5

6

7

8

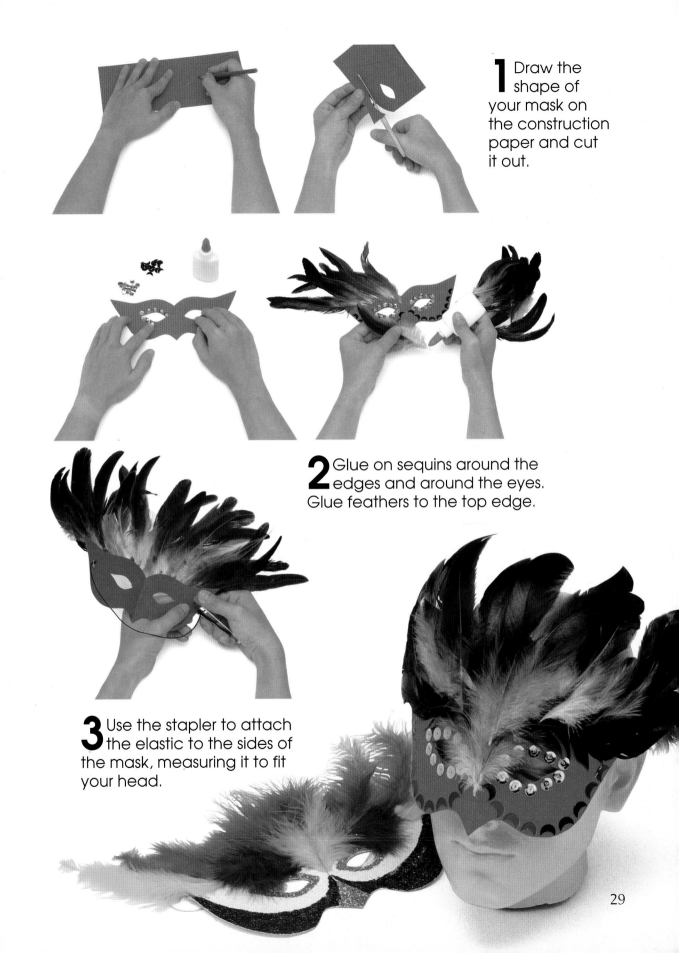

1 Draw the shape of your mask on the construction paper and cut it out.

2 Glue on sequins around the edges and around the eyes. Glue feathers to the top edge.

3 Use the stapler to attach the elastic to the sides of the mask, measuring it to fit your head.

29

MAKE PIZZA

D o you like pizza? Have you ever made your own? It's not all that hard to do, and it tastes even better than the kind you buy. Try it!

You will need:
1. 1 cup (115 g) flour
2. 1 teaspoon baking powder
3. ¼ teaspoon salt
4. ⅓ cup (80 ml) milk
5. ⅛ cup (30 ml) plus 1 tablespoon salad oil
6. ¼ cup (25 g) grated parmesan cheese
7. 4 ounces (115 g) tomato sauce
8. ½ tablespoon chopped onions
9. ¼ teaspoon oregano
10. ⅛ teaspoon pepper
11. ¼ pound (115 g) shredded mozzarella cheese
12. ¼ cup (50 g) sliced mushrooms
13. ⅛ cup (25 g) sliced pitted olives
14. Measuring cups
15. Measuring spoons
16. Mixing bowl
17. Knife
18. Pizza pan or baking sheet
19. Wooden spoon
20. Cutting board
21. Potholder
22. Sifter

4

6 and 14

5

2

7

13

1 and 16

12

8

9

11, 18 and 21

3

15

10

17, 19, 20 and 22

1 Sift flour. Measure flour, baking powder, salt, milk, and ⅛ cup salad oil into bowl. Stir until mixture leaves side of bowl.

2 Gather dough together and press into a ball. Knead dough 10 times to make it smooth.

3 Press the dough into pizza pan or baking sheet. Turn up edge a little bit all around. Brush with salad oil.

4 Layer pizza toppings in order listed. Bake at 425°F (220°C) for 20–25 minutes. Cut into wedges and eat!

31

GLOSSARY

confraternity, 16   A group of people who do work for charity.
contrada, 8   A neighborhood, the center of a community.
crucifixion, 16   Being put to death on the cross.
gondola, 5   A long boat rowed by a boatman at the back, called a gondolier.
martyred, 21   To be killed because of one's religious beliefs.
maschera nobile, 12   Noblemen's mask; the traditional costume at Venice Carnival.
Middle Ages, 22   A time 400–900 years ago, when there were knights and kings.
peninsula, 4   A piece of land that sticks out into the water.
piazza, 10   Square; the open area in the center of a town.
plague, 6   A disease that spreads and kills many people.
Renaissance, 4   A time after the Middle Ages, when there were many advances in science and art.
resurrection, 16   The miracle of coming back to life.
Sior Maschera, 15   "Sir Mask," the name given to Carnival participants.
trade guilds, 16   Old organizations of workers in a particular craft.

INDEX

This book may be kept
FOURTEEN DAYS
A fine will be charged for each
day the book is kept overtime.

FEB 1 2 2001 NOV 1 9 2013			